Cambridge Young Learners English Tests

Cambridge Starters 3

Examination papers from

University of Cambridge
ESOL Examinations:

English for Speakers of Other Languages

CAMBRIDGE UNIVERSITY PRESS
Cambridge, New York, Melbourne, Madrid, Cape Town,
Singapore, São Paulo, Delhi, Tokyo, Mexico City

Cambridge University Press
The Edinburgh Building, Cambridge CB2 8RU, UK

www.cambridge.org
Information on this title: www.cambridge.org/9780521693608

© Cambridge University Press 2007

This publication is in copyright. Subject to statutory exception
and to the provisions of relevant collective licensing agreements,
no reproduction of any part may take place without the written
permission of Cambridge University Press.

First published 2003
5th printing 2011

Printed in the United Kingdom at the University Press, Cambridge

A catalogue record for this publication is available from the British Library

ISBN 978-0-521-69360-8 Student's Book
ISBN 978-0-521-69361-5 Answer Booklet
ISBN 978-0-521-69362-2 Cassette
ISBN 978-0-521-69363-9 CD (audio)

Cover design by David Lawton
Produced by HL Studios

Cambridge University Press has no responsibility for the persistence or
accuracy of URLs for external or third-party internet websites referred to in
this publication, and does not guarantee that any content on such websites is,
or will remain, accurate or appropriate. Information regarding prices, travel
timetables and other factual information given in this work is correct at
the time of first printing but Cambridge University Press does not guarantee
the accuracy of such information thereafter.

Contents

Test 1
Listening — 5
Reading and Writing — 11

Test 2
Listening — 19
Reading and Writing — 25

Test 3
Listening — 33
Reading and Writing — 39

Speaking Tests
Test 1 — 47
Test 2 — 51
Test 3 — 55

Test 1
Listening

Part 1
– 5 questions –

Listen and draw lines. There is one example.

Part 2
– 5 questions –

Read the question. Listen and write a name or a number.

There are two examples.

Examples

What's the girl's name? ....Alex.................

How old is she? ....7..................

Questions

1 How many brothers does Alex have?   ....

2 Who is Alex's friend?   ....

3 How many children are in the class?   ....

4 How old is the mouse?   ....

5 What's the name of Alex's teacher?   Mr ....

Part 3
– 5 questions –

Listen and tick (✔) the box. There is one example.

What's John drinking?

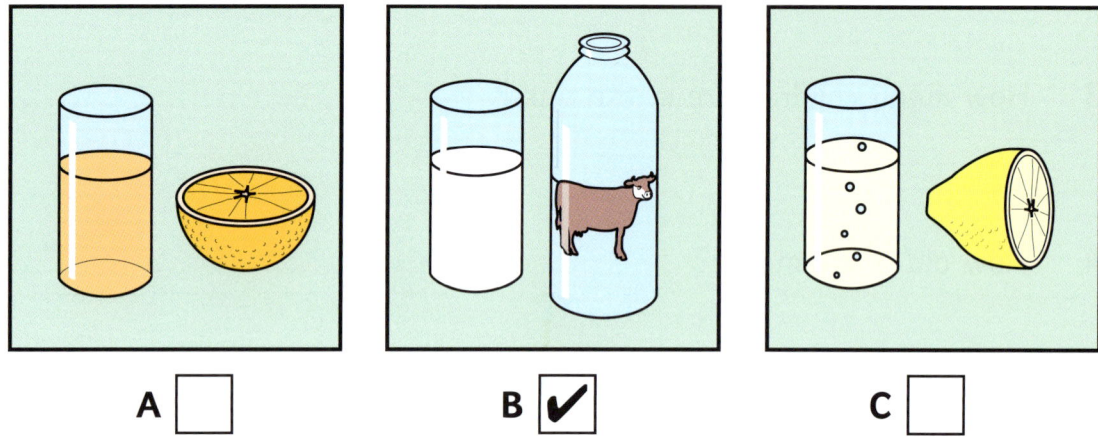

1   Which boy is Sam?

2   Which is Ann's new dress?

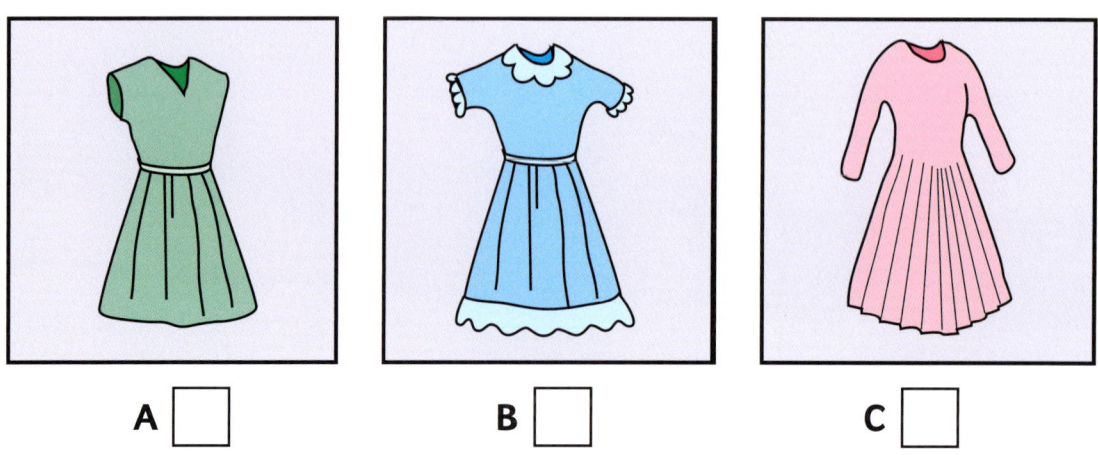

3 Which monster does Sam like?

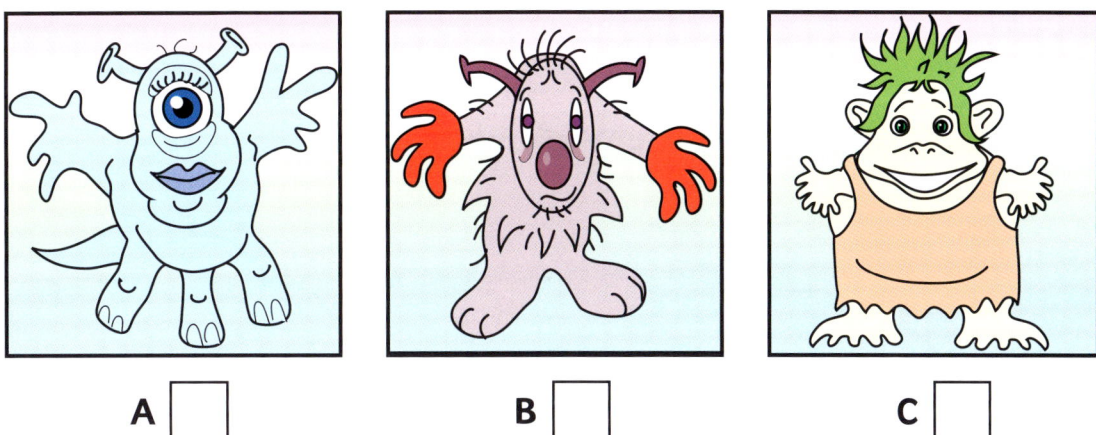

A ☐   B ☐   C ☐

4 How does Bill go to school?

A ☐   B ☐   C ☐

5 What's for supper?

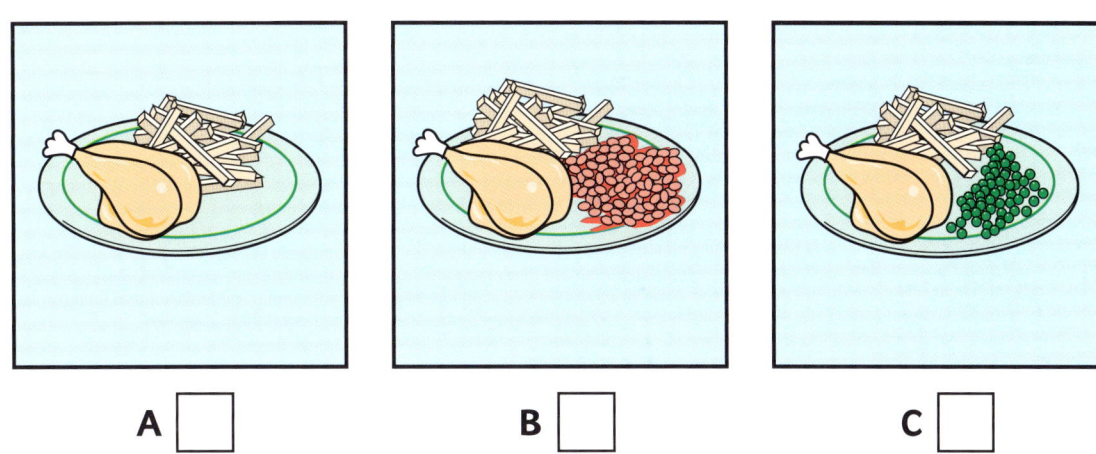

A ☐   B ☐   C ☐

Test 1

Part 4
– 5 questions –

Listen and colour. There is one example.

Test 1
Reading and Writing

Part 1
– 5 questions –

Look and read. Put a tick (✓) or a cross (✗) in the box.
There are two examples.

Examples

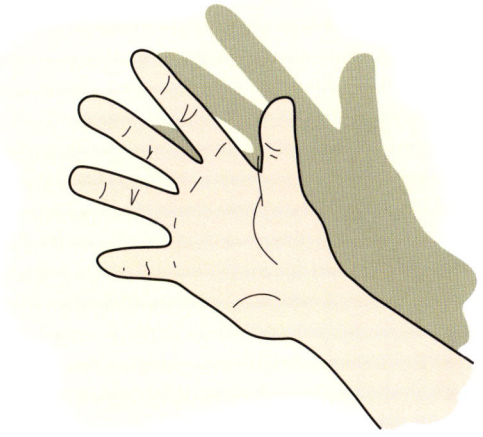

This is a hand.

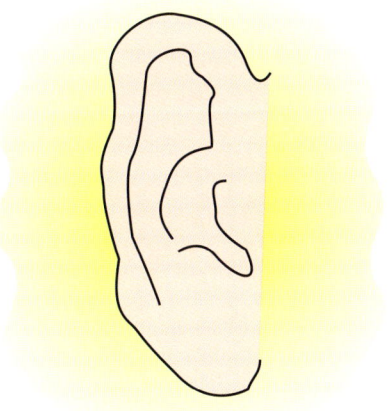

This is an eye.

Questions

1

This is a hippo.

Test 1

2   This is a bookcase. ☐

3   This is a chicken. ☐

4   This is a chair. ☐

5   This is a plane. ☐

Reading and Writing

Part 2
– 5 questions –

Look and read. Write yes or no.

Examples

The boy is wearing a hat.	..............yes..............
There are four frogs in the water.	..............no..............

Questions

1 The boy's trousers are yellow. ....

2 There is a duck next to the boy. ....

3 The boy is playing with a toy plane. ....

4 There is a bird in the boat. ....

5 The boy's feet are in the water. ....

Part 3
– 5 questions –

Look at the pictures. Look at the letters. Write the words.

Example

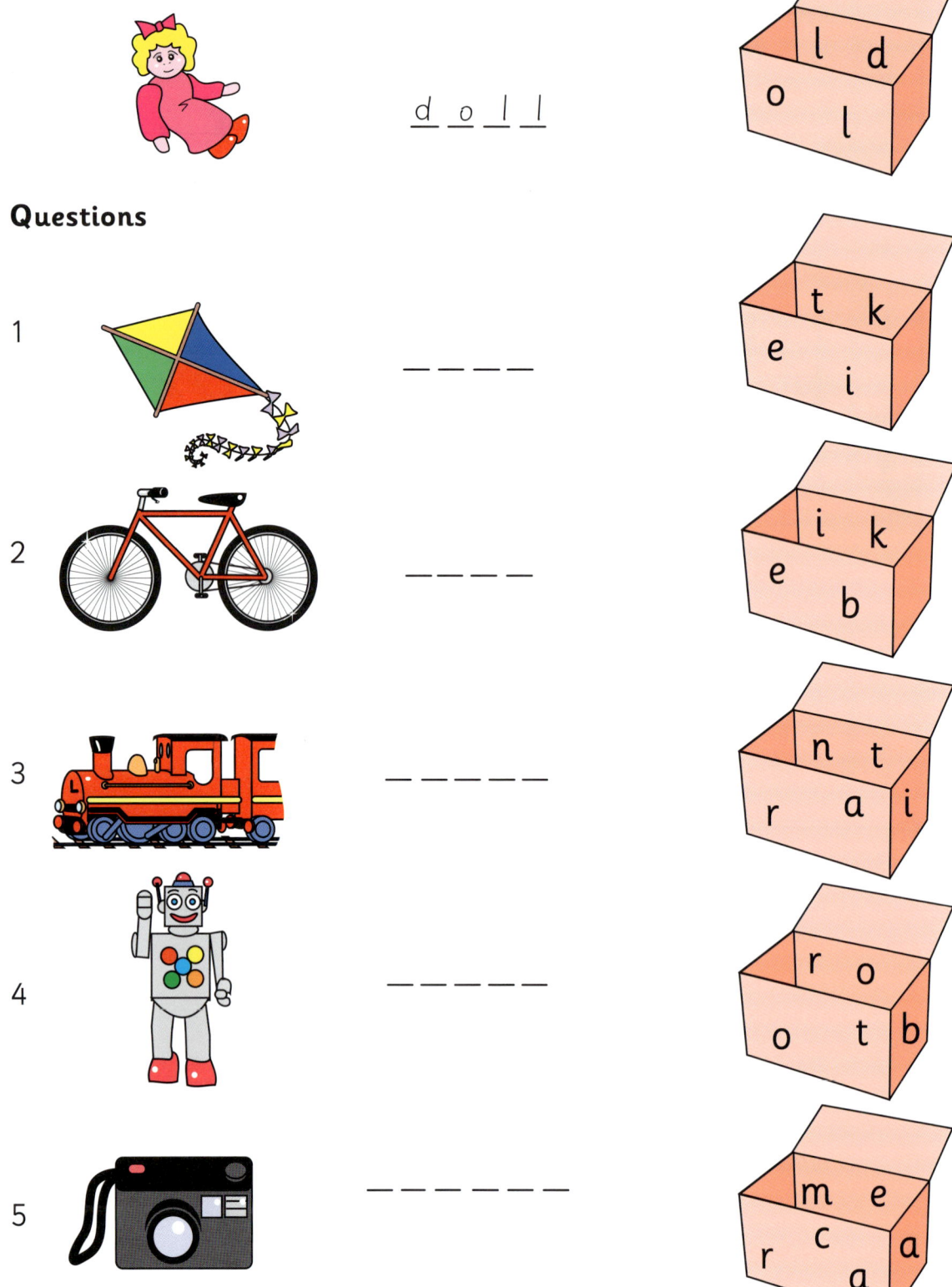

d o l l

Questions

1 _ _ _ _

2 _ _ _ _

3 _ _ _ _ _

4 _ _ _ _

5 _ _ _ _ _ _

Part 4
– 5 questions –

Read this. Choose a word from the box. Write the correct word next to numbers 1–5. There is one example.

A desk

I am in a ...classroom... in Lucy's school. Lucy's teacher sits on a

(1) .... in front of me. Lucy can see his legs and

(2) .... under me! He puts his ruler, **(3)** .... and

pencils on me. The **(4)** .... stand next to me, and Lucy's

teacher looks at their books. I am like a **(5)** .... but people

don't sit and eat breakfast at me.

What am I? I am a desk.

Part 5
– 5 questions –

Look at the pictures and read the questions. Write one-word answers.

Examples

What is on the table next to the bed?   a .... lamp ....

What is the cat doing?   .... sleeping ....

Questions

1   Which room is Sue in?   her ....

Reading and Writing

2   Where is Sue now?   in the ....

3   What is Sue eating?   an ....

4   What is the cat drinking?   ....

5   What colour is the sun?   ....

Blank Page

Test 2
Listening

Part 1
– 5 questions –

Listen and draw lines. There is one example.

Test 2

Part 2
– 5 questions –

Read the question. Listen and write a name or a number.

There are two examples.

Examples

What's the girl's name? ....Anna............

How old is she? ....8..............

Questions

1 What's the name of Anna's school? ....Tree School

2 How many children are in Anna's class? ....

3 Who sits next to Anna at school? ....

4 What's the name of Anna's English teacher? ....

5 How many monsters are in the story? ....

Part 3
– 5 questions –

Listen and tick (✔) the box. There is one example.

What's Sue doing?

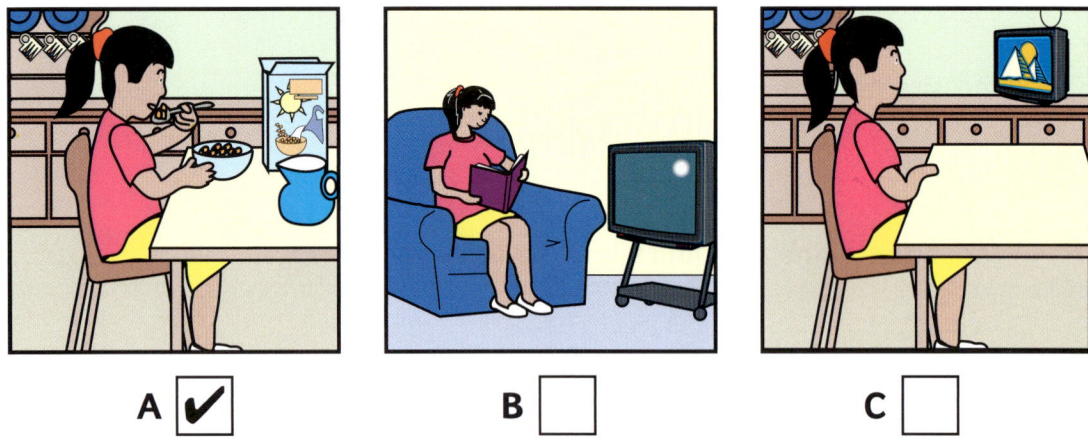

1   What's Tom's favourite animal?

2   Where's the baby?

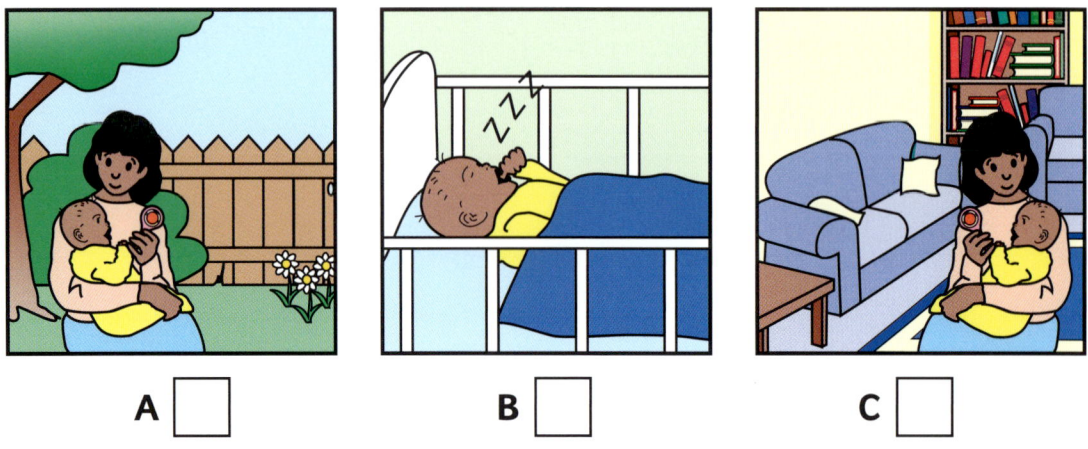

3   What's Ben having for lunch?

4   Which girl is Kim?

5   What does Nick want for his birthday?

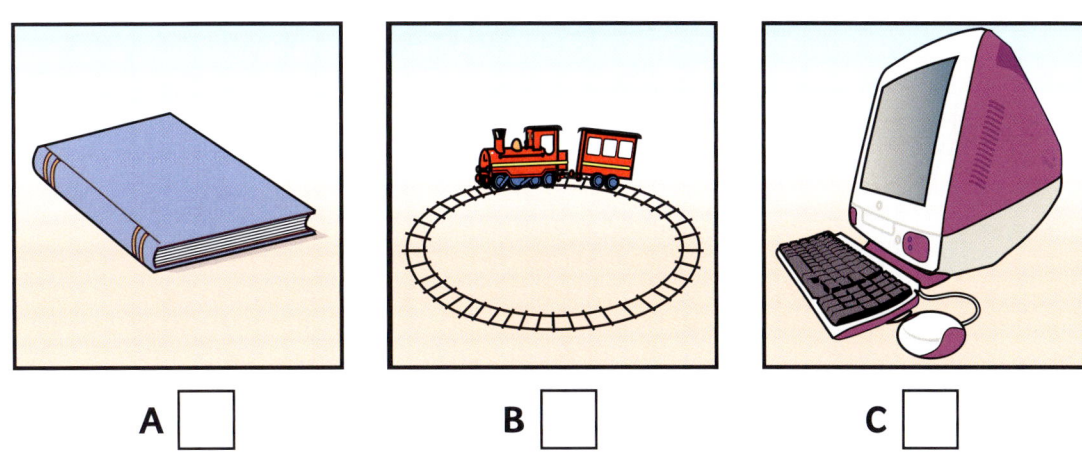

Part 4
– 5 questions –

Listen and colour. There is one example.

Test 2
Reading and Writing

Part 1
– 5 questions –

Look and read. Put a tick (✓) or a cross (✗) in the box.
There are two examples.

Examples

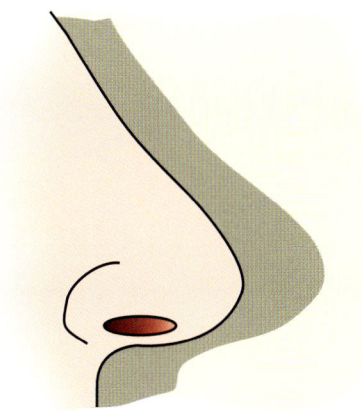

This is a nose.

This is a piano.

Questions

1

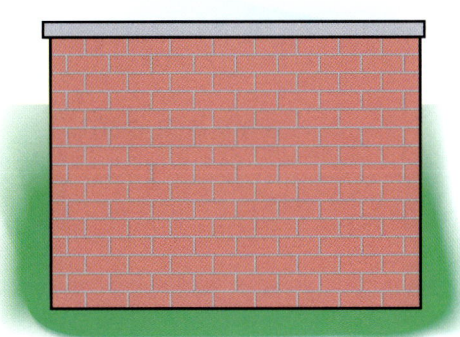

This is a wall.

Test 2

2

This is a kitchen. ☐

3

This is a dress. ☐

4

This is a T-shirt. ☐

5

This is a goat. ☐

Part 2
– 5 questions –

Look and read. Write yes or no.

Examples

There are two cars in the picture.   yes

A man is riding a horse.   no

Questions

1 The man in the red jacket is
   wearing short trousers.   ....

2 A girl is bouncing some balls.   ....

3 There's a kite in a tree.   ....

4 There's a monkey on the motorbike. ....

5 The woman in the blue car is singing. ....

Part 3
– 5 questions –

Look at the pictures. Look at the letters. Write the words.

Example

p i c t u r e

Questions

1

_ _ _ _ _

2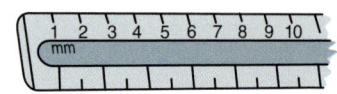

_ _ _ _ _ _

3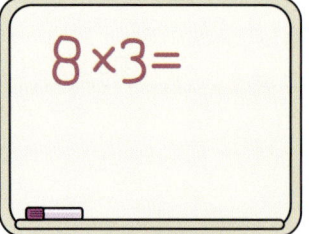

_ _ _ _ _

4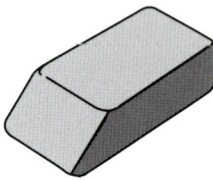

_ _ _ _ _ _

5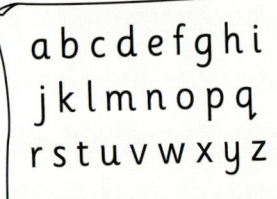

_ _ _ _ _ _ _ _

Part 4
– 5 questions –

Read this. Choose a word from the box. Write the correct word next to numbers 1–5. There is one example.

A phone

I have very small ....letters.... and **(1)** .... from 0 to 9 on me.

You can find me on a table in a **(2)** .... People hold me in

their **(3)** .... , and put part of me next to their

(4) .... Then they can talk and listen to their friends.

Some **(5)** .... go to school with me in their school bags.

What am I? I am a phone.

Part 5
– 5 questions –

Look at the pictures and read the questions. Write one-word answers.

Examples

What is the girl doing? …………reading…………

Where is the girl's mother? at the ………door………

Questions

1 Where are the clothes? on the ………………………

Reading and Writing

2   Where is the girl putting
    the clothes?   under the ....

3   How many books are there
    in the bookcase?   ....

4   What is the girl eating?   some ....

5   What is the girl's mother picking up? a ....

Blank Page

Test 3
Listening

Part 1
– 5 questions –

Listen and draw lines. There is one example.

 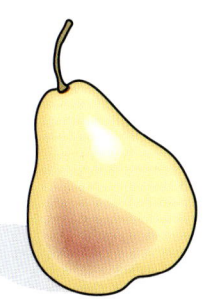 

Test 3

Part 2
– 5 questions –

Read the question. Listen and write a name or a number.

There are two examples.

Examples

What's the girl's name? ....May.................

How old is she? ....10.................

Questions

1 What's the name of May's sister? ....

2 Where does May live? .... Street

3 What number is May's house? ....

4 What's the name of May's grandfather? Mr ....

5 How many children are in May's class? ....

Part 3
− 5 questions −

Listen and tick (✔) the box. There is one example.

What's Pat's favourite food?

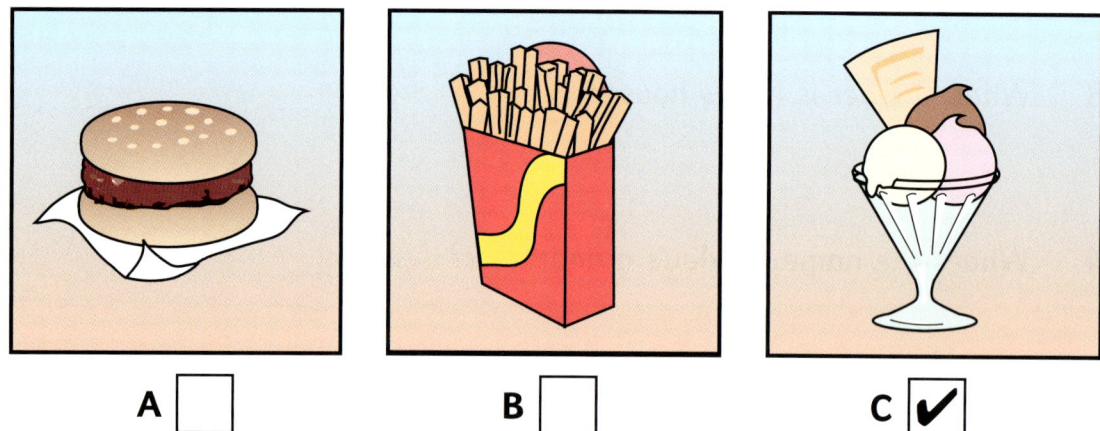

1 Who is Ben's teacher?

2 Which colour does Mum like?

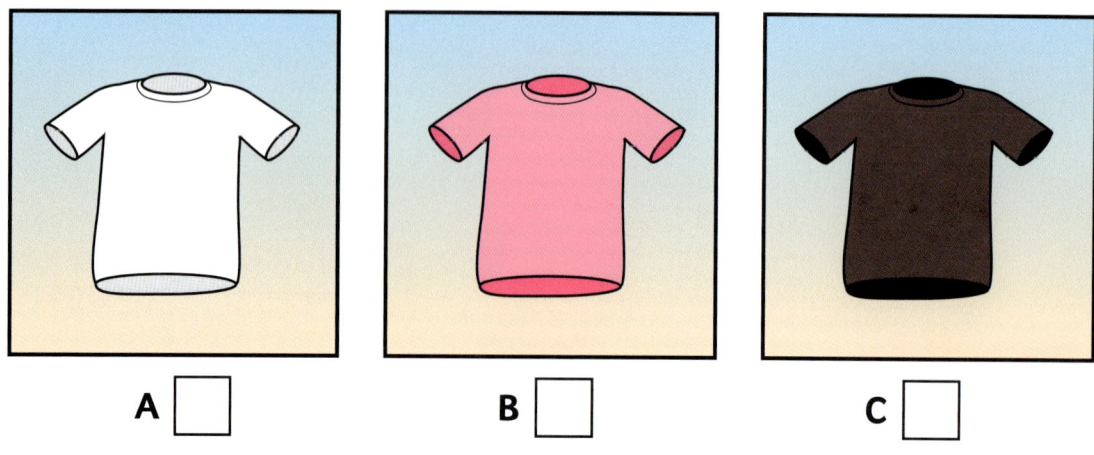

Listening

3   Which boy is Tom?

A ☐   B ☐   C ☐

4   Where are Kim's jeans?

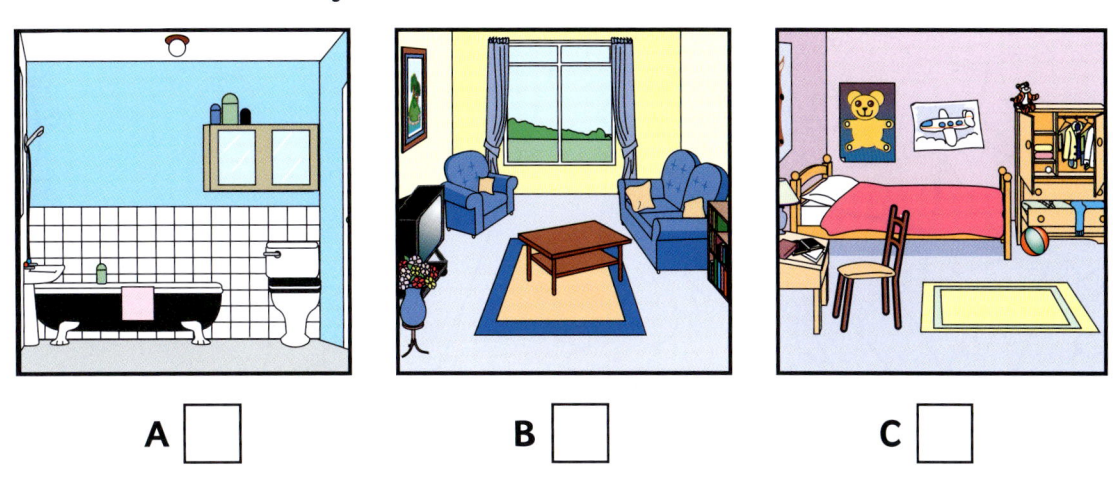

A ☐   B ☐   C ☐

5   What does Bill want for his breakfast?

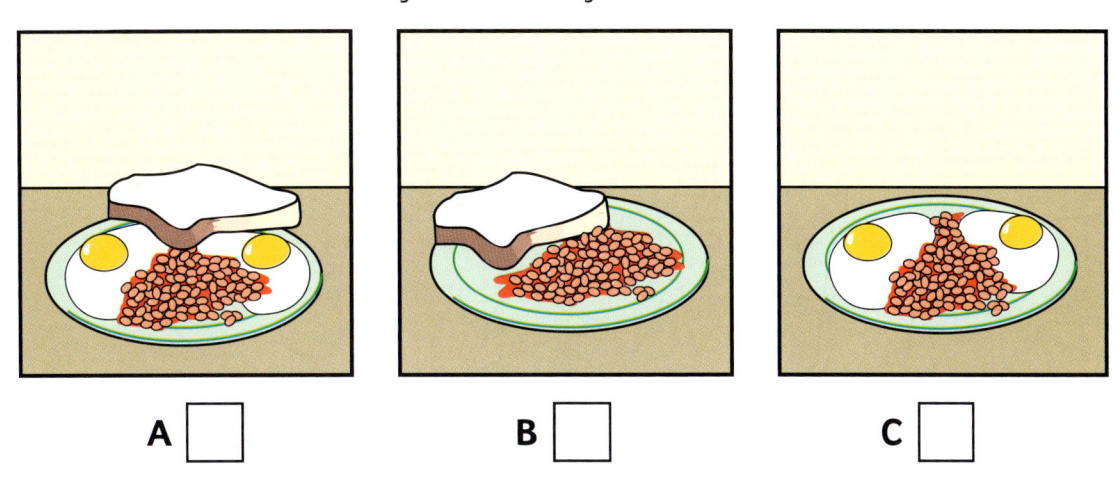

A ☐   B ☐   C ☐

Test 3

Part 4
– 5 questions –

Listen and colour. There is one example.

Test 3
Reading and Writing

Part 1
– 5 questions –

Look and read. Put a tick (✔) or a cross (✗) in the box.
There are two examples.

Examples

This is a mouse. ✔

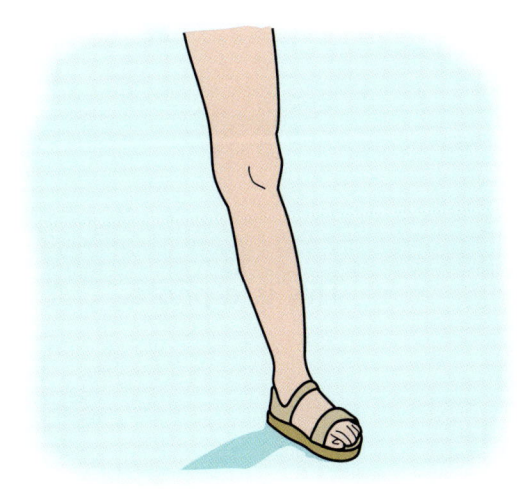

This is an arm. ✗

Questions

1. This is a pear. ☐

Test 3

2   This is a television. ☐

3   This is a page. ☐

4   This is a photo. ☐

5   This is a shirt. ☐

40

Part 2
– 5 questions –

Look and read. Write yes or no.

Examples

The man is eating a burger. ....yes.................

The dog has got a sausage. ....no.................

Questions

1 The woman is standing at the window. ....

2 There's a radio under the chair. ....

3 Two children are playing table tennis. ....

4 There are two birds in the big tree. ....

5 The boy is bouncing a ball. ....

Part 3
– 5 questions –

Look at the pictures. Look at the letters. Write the words.

Example

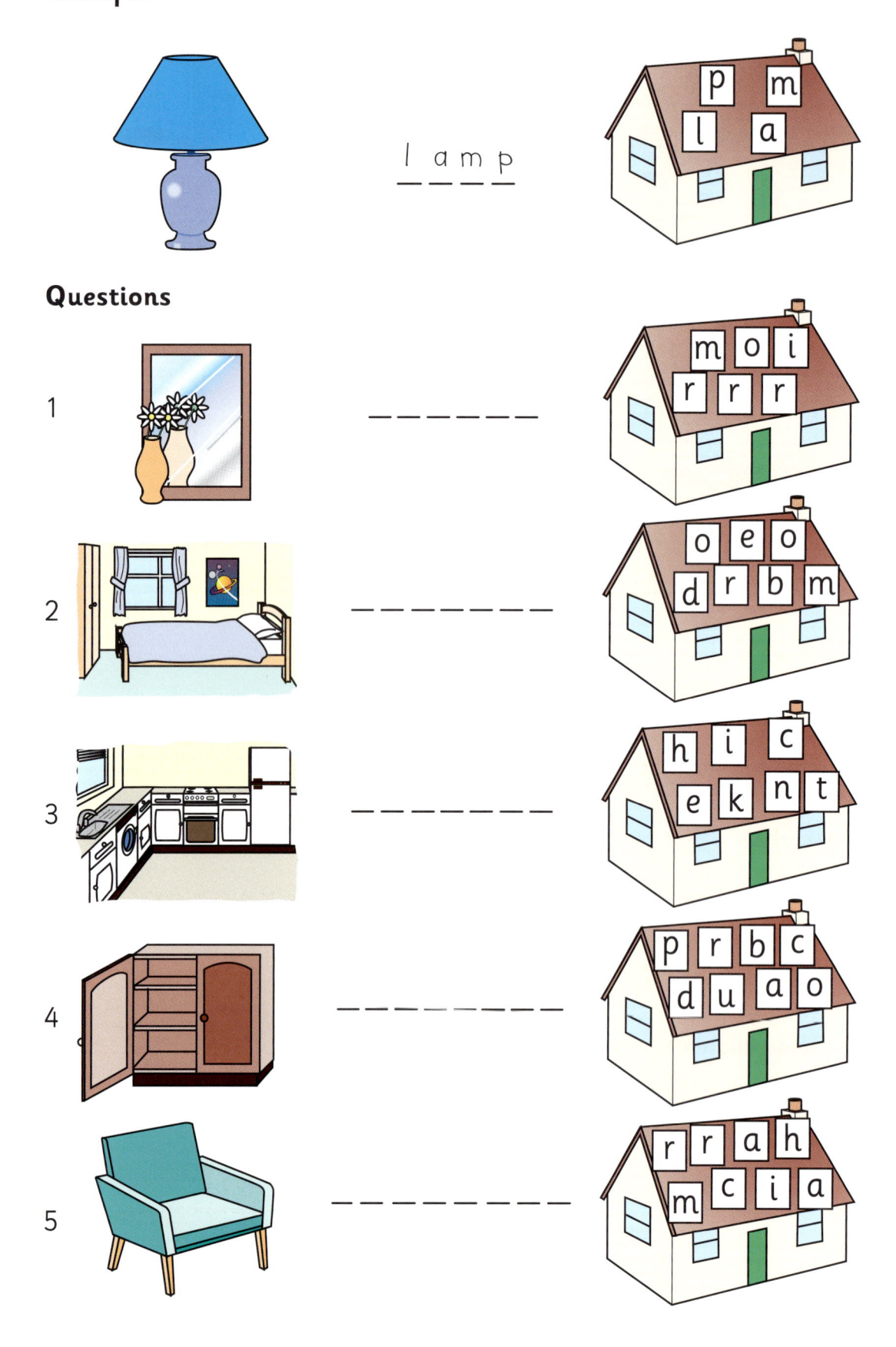

l a m p

Questions

1 _ _ _ _ _ _

2 _ _ _ _ _ _

3 _ _ _ _ _ _

4 _ _ _ _ _ _

5 _ _ _ _ _ _

Reading and Writing

Part 4
– 5 questions –

Read this. Choose a word from the box. Write the correct word next to numbers 1–5. There is one example.

A school

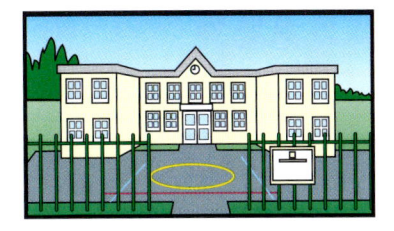

Boys and .....*girls*..... come and learn in me. There are lots of

classrooms in me and some children have **(1)** .... in

English here. In one classroom, Lucy sits on her **(2)** .... , opens

her **(3)** .... and writes in it with her pen. There are lots of

(4) .... on the wall. Lucy and her friends draw them with

their **(5)** .... The children are happy here.

What am I? I am a school.

example: girls | lessons | pencils | chair | pictures | ice cream | book | drink

Test 3

Part 5
– 5 questions –

Look at the pictures and read the questions. Write one-word answers.

Examples

What are the children standing next to?   the .... shop ....

What colour is the bus?   .... yellow ....

Questions

1   How many children are there in the picture?   ....

Reading and Writing

2   Who is talking on the phone?   the ....

3   Where are the girls now?   on the ....

4   What has the man got in his hand?   a ....

5   What are the boys pointing at?   some ....

Blank Page

Test 1
Speaking

SCENE CARD

Blank Page

OBJECT CARDS

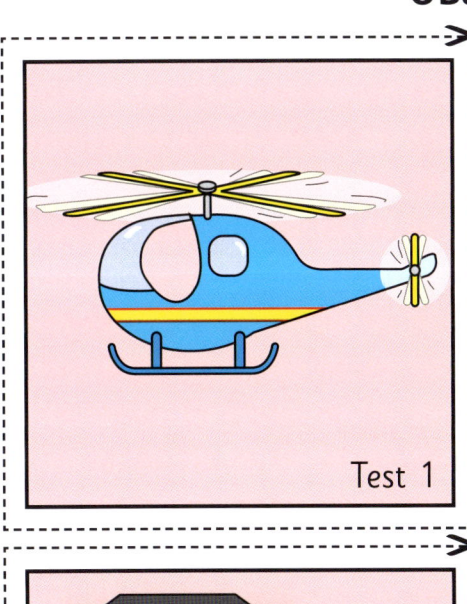

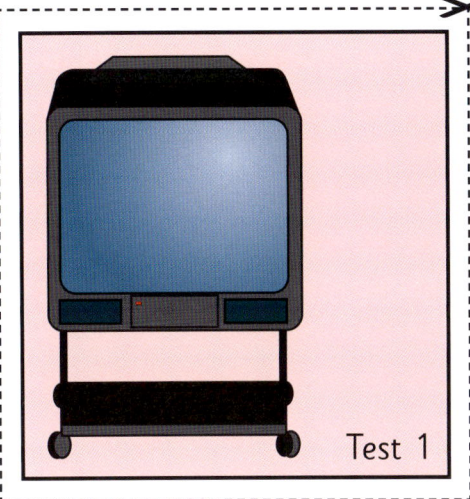

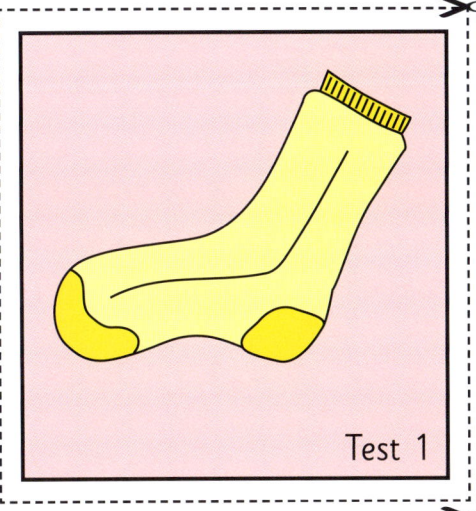

Test 1 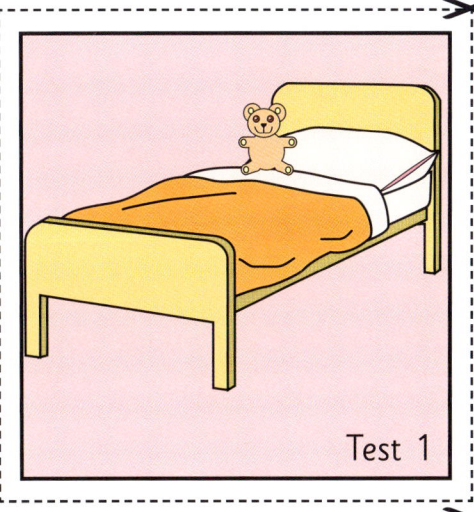 — Test 1
Test 1  — Test 1
Test 1 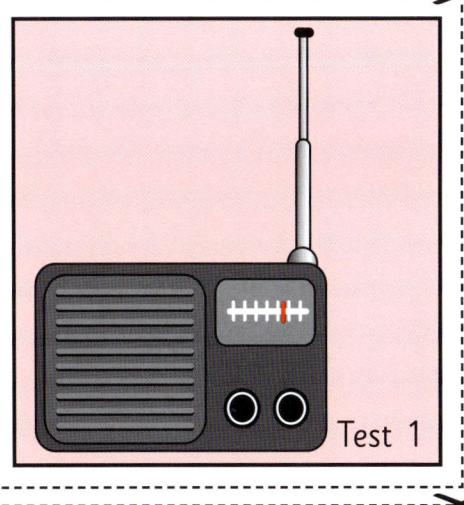 — Test 1
Test 1  — Test 1

Blank Page

Test 2
Speaking

SCENE CARD

Blank Page

OBJECT CARDS

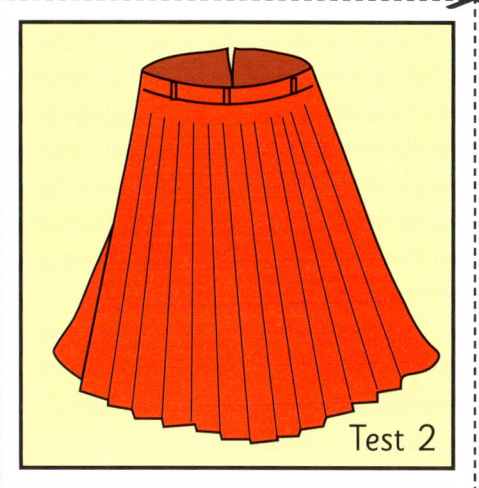

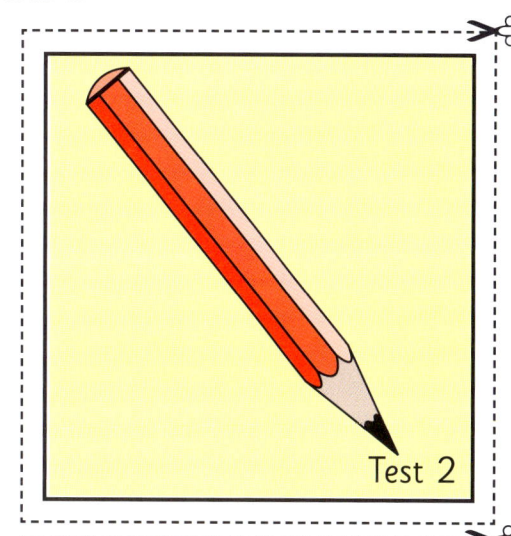

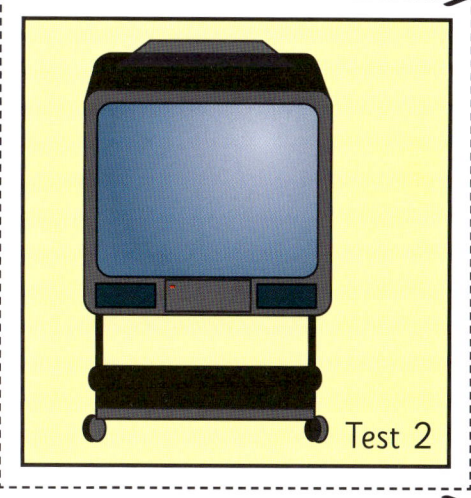

53

Blank Page

Test 3
Speaking

SCENE CARD

Blank Page

OBJECT CARDS

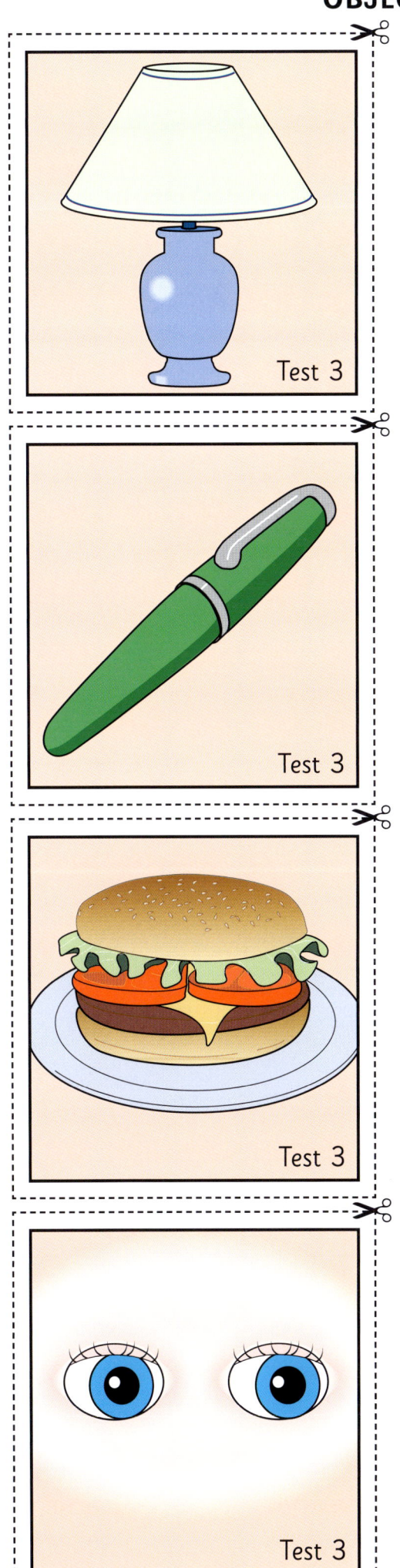

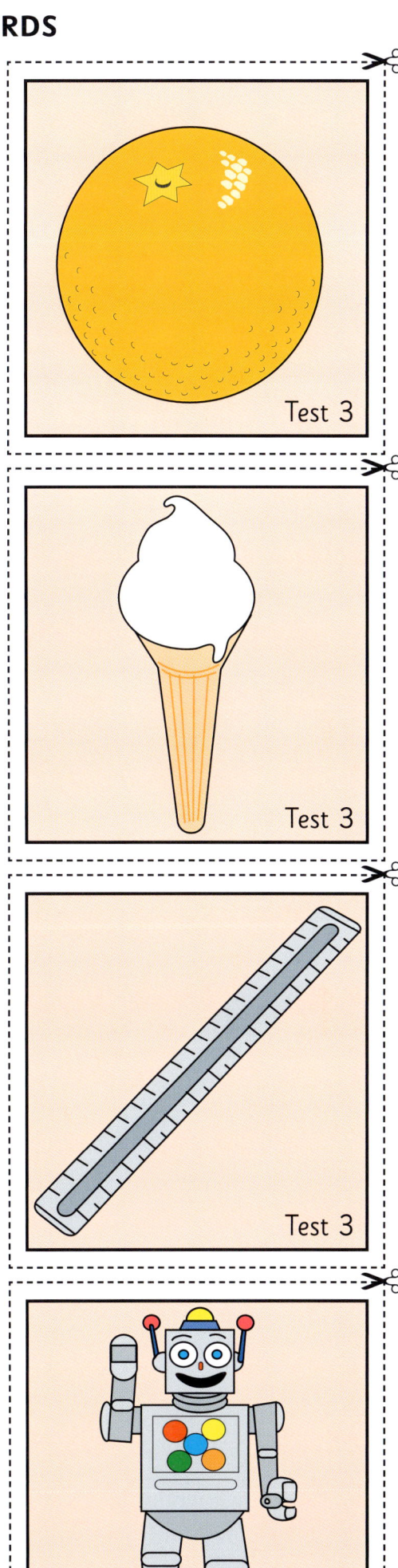

Test 3 — Test 3
Test 3 — Test 3
Test 3 — Test 3
Test 3 — Test 3